Lord, keep us safe this night,
Secure from all our fears;
May angels guard us while we sleep,
Till morning light appears.
John Leland (1754—1841)

This book belongs to

To:
Natalya Cannon

with love from Auntie

LeAnne, Uncle Ray & Vaughn ♡

Happy. Third Birthday Taly!
1999

Text by Lois Rock
Illustrations copyright © 1997 Illustrator Louise Rawlings
This edition copyright © 1997 Lion Publishing
The author asserts the moral right
to be identified as the author of this work
Published by
Lion Publishing plc
Sandy Lane West, Oxford, England
ISBN 0 7459 3616 4
Lion Publishing
4050 Lee Vance View, Colorado Springs, CO 80918, USA
ISBN 0 7459 3616 4
First edition 1997
10 9 8 7 6 5 4 3 2 1 0
Acknowledgments
A catalogue record for this book is available
from the British Library
Printed and bound in Singapore

NIGHTLIGHTS

Safe This Night

Lois Rock

ILLUSTRATED BY LOUISE RAWLINGS

A LION BOOK

The day is nearly over,
The day is almost done:
Just think of all that's happened
Since the rising of the sun.

Think of the
morning light.
It makes me happy.

Think of the bright
daytime.
It makes me happy.

Think of the golden
afternoon.
It makes me happy.

The sun must shine on other lands
And soon it will be night.
Think of all the things you saw
When everything was light.

Think of the earth
and the water.
**what a wonderful
world.**

Think of the sun
and sky.
**what a wonderful
world.**

Think of the plants
and animals.
**what a wonderful
world.**

Think of all the people
who helped you on your way,
Who gave you things you needed,
Who helped with work and play.

Think of kind things
done by people who
seem very grand.
I am glad that
I am loved.

Think of kind things
done by people you
know well.
I am glad that
I am loved.

Think of kind things
done by little people
like you.
I am glad that
I am loved.

Think of all the good things
That you have learned to do:
The things that make you special
And glad that you are you.

In making and
doing
I'm glad to be me.

In talking and
singing
I'm glad to be me.

In laughing and
loving
I'm glad to be me.

Perhaps today there were some things
That you did not get right.
So say goodbye to old mistakes
And put them out of sight.

Sometimes I hurt things:
Later I want things put right.

Sometimes I say angry words:
Later I want things put right.

Sometimes I want to scream and shout at the whole world:
Later I want things put right.

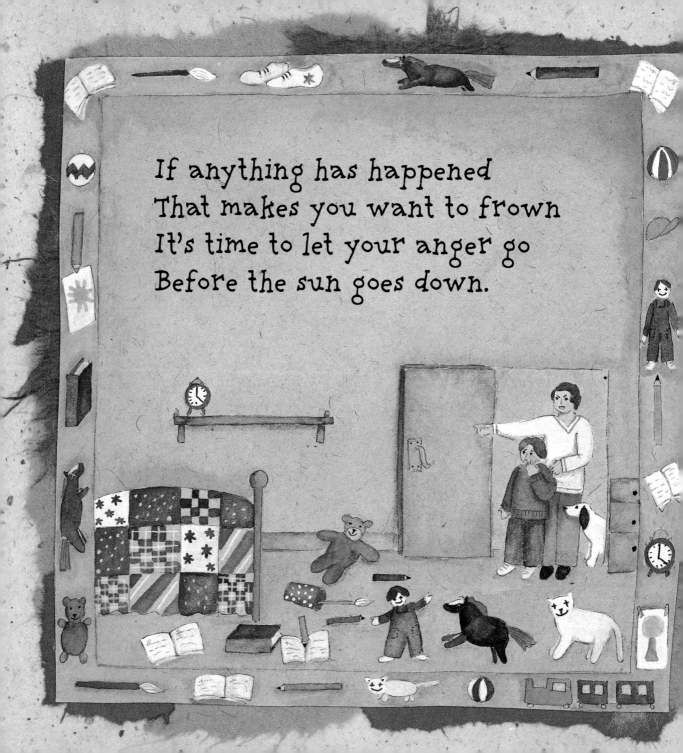

If anything has happened
That makes you want to frown
It's time to let your anger go
Before the sun goes down.

Any sad tears:
Go away now.

Any angry thoughts:
Go away now.

Any nasty plans:
Go away now.

You can be sure that God is close
All through the long, dark night;
That you are safe in God's great love
And always in God's sight.

When darkness falls
Dear God, be near me.

When I feel alone
Dear God, be near me.

If I feel scared
Dear God, be near me.

Believe that God will hear your prayers
For people good and bad;
And join in all their happiness,
And weep when they are sad.

Some people are
happy tonight.
Be close to them,
dear God.

Some people are
sad tonight.
Be close to them,
dear God.

Some people are
in need tonight.
Be close to them,
dear God.

The world tonight is safe with God,
The God who does not sleep;
The birds, the plants, the animals,
The creatures of the deep.

watch over your world
And the plants and creatures that rest in the dark hours.

watch over your world
And the plants and creatures that wake in the dark hours.

watch over your world
And hold it safe between its sun, moon and stars.

Now tell God what you hope for:
For love and joy and light
To fill all your tomorrows.

Make tomorrow
a good day
and show your
love to us.

Make tomorrow
a good day
and help us to
love you more.

Make tomorrow
a good day
and help us to
show your love
to others.

And so to bed:
Goodnight.